Discovering My World

From Tadpole to Frog

by Melvin and Gilda Berger

S0-ACC-634

SCHOLASTIC INC.

New York   Toronto   London   Auckland
Sydney   Mexico City   New Delhi   Hong Kong

ISBN 978-0-545-24451-0

12 11 10 9 8 7 6 5 4 3 2   11 12 13 14 15 16/0

Printed in the U.S.A.   40
First printing, April 2011

Photo Credits:

Cover: © Media Bakery; Back cover: © blickwinkel/Alamy; Title page: © Hans Pfletschinger/Photolibrary; Page 3: © Media Bakery; Page 4: © Denis Bringard/Photolibrary; Page 5: © Robin Monchâtre/Photolibrary; Page 6: © Chris Mattison/Alamy; Page 7: © Zigmund Leszcynski/Animals Animals; Page 8: © Robin Smith/Getty Images; Page 9: © Photoshot Holdings Ltd/Alamy; Page 10: © DHarms DHarms/Photolibrary; Page 11: © Media Bakery; Page 12: © Michel Rauch/Photolibrary; Page 13: © Joe McDonald/Corbis; Page 14: © Tom Lazar/Animals Animals; Page 15: © Oxford Scientific/Photolibrary; Page 16: © Media Bakery

Frogs live in water and on land.

Are the eggs round?

Most frogs lay their eggs in water.

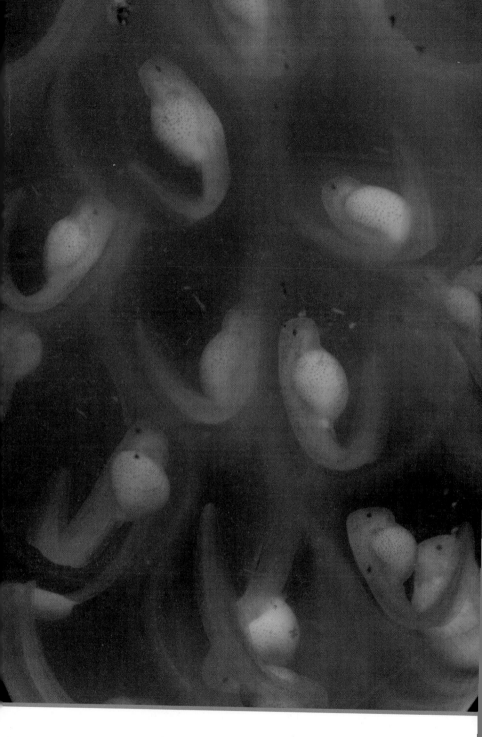

The eggs hatch.

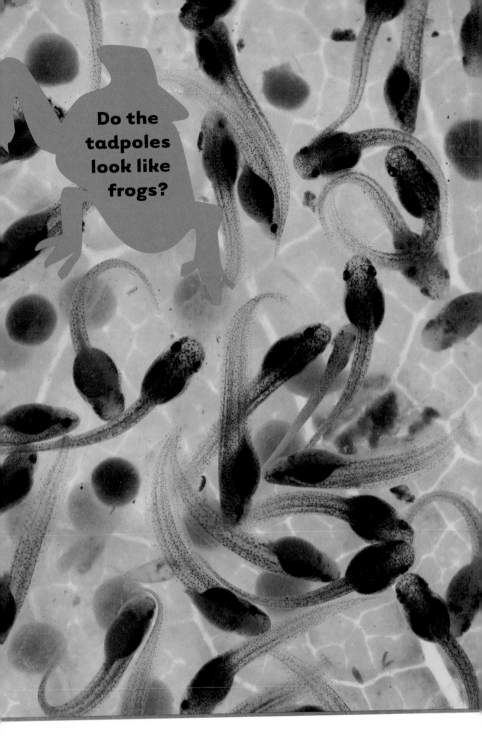

Tadpoles come out.

The tadpoles have tails, but no legs.

Soon the tadpoles grow back legs.

Then they grow front legs.

Next the tail grows smaller.

What color is the young frog?

The young frog leaves the water.

Some frogs eat insects.

Some frogs eat worms.

Are this frog's eyes above the water?

Frogs swim.

Frogs jump!

Ask Yourself

1. Where do frogs live?
2. Where do most frogs lay their eggs?
3. What hatches from the eggs?
4. Are tadpoles born with legs?
5. Do frogs jump?

You can find the answers in this book.